77 High Impact Low Budget Tips to Sell More Mattresses Easily

By

Jeff Giagnocavo

© 2017 Infotail Systems, Inc.

Any unauthorized use, sharing, reproduction or distribution of these materials by any means, electronic, mechanical, or otherwise is strictly prohibited. No portion of these materials may be reproduced in any manner whatsoever, without the express written consent of the publisher.

Published under the Copyright Laws of the Library of Congress of The United States of America, by:

Infotail Systems, Inc.
470 Boot Rd. #688
Downingtown, PA 19335

While all attempts have been made to verify information provided in this publication, neither the author nor the publisher assumes any responsibility for errors, omissions or contradictory interpretation of the subject matter herein. This publication is not intended to be used as a source of legal or accounting advice. Please remember that the information contained may be subject to varying state and/or local laws or regulations that may apply to the user's particular practice.

The purchaser or reader of this publication assumes responsibility for the use of these materials and information. Adherence to all applicable laws and regulations, both federal, state, and local, governing professional licensing, business practices, advertising and any other aspects of doing business in the United States or any other jurisdiction is the sole responsibility of the purchaser or reader. Infotail Systems, Inc. assumes no responsibility or liability whatsoever on behalf of any purchaser or reader of these materials. Any perceived slights of specific people or organizations are unintentional. 090117.

Table of Contents

Foreword by Dale T. Read	1
Introduction	5
A Few Words from Dan Kennedy	9
Part 1: Must Do Tips	11
1. Realize You Have Five Types of People In Your Business	12
2. Your Job is Not Selling Mattresses, It's Marketing	15
3. Always Be Marketing	16
4. Evaluate and Monitor Every Marketing Effort	17
5. Have a Unique Selling Position	18
6. Clearly Define Your Mission	19
7. Have a System for Everything	20
8. Develop a Sales Process & Choreography	21
9. Educate Your Customers as to the Value You Offer	22
10. Understand Your #1 Product is YOU!	23
11. Build Your #1 Asset - Your List	24
12. Always Capture Name and Email	25
13. Always Follow Up With Everybody!	26
14. Always Ask for a Response & Provide a Way to Respond	27
15. Always Have an Offer & Deadline	28
16. Offer a Rock Solid Guarantee	29
17. Fire Yourself	30
18. Stop Being Your Own Assistant	31

19. Hire Eagles, Not Turkeys	32
20. Have a Website that Engages Your Customer	33
21. Use Video to Direct Traffic & Increase Opt-ins	34
22. Raise Your Prices & Profit	35
23. Address the "Payment Elephant" in the Room	36
24. Ask for Referrals	37
25. Negotiate Ad Rates on Your Terms	38
26. Host an Anniversary Event	39
27. Make it Right	40

Part 2: Should Do Tips — 41

28. Use a CRM System	42
29. Create and Maintain a Marketing Calendar	43
30. Create Your Own Marketing Library	44
31. Test New Marketing Ideas Frequently	45
32. Resurrect Promotions that Have Worked in the Past	46
33. Publish a Customer Newsletter	47
34. Create and Give WOW! Packages	48
35. Use Stories in Your Marketing	49
36. Use Giveaways to Attract New Customers	50
37. Use Testimonials the Right Way	51
38. Become a Trusted Advisor, Write a Column	52
39. Become a Trusted Authority, Write a Book	53
40. Be an Award Winner in Your Community	54
41. Make Your Own Currency	55
42. Have Fun - Turn Yourself Into a Cartoon	56

43. Send Birthday and Anniversary Cards 57

44. Got a Story to Tell? Tell Your Local Paper About It! 58

45. Do Something Charitable in Your Community 59

46. Offer Fun and Educational Workshops 60

47. Interview Customers After Purchase 61

48. Write Blog Posts for Search Engine Optimization 62

49. Put a Unique Marketing Message on Your Truck 63

50. Don't Be Afraid to Offer Long Term Financing 64

51. Steer Clear of Price Games and Deception 65

52. Offer Sleep Assessments 66

53. Diversify, Don't be Dependent on One Brand 67

54. Dig Deep On Your Local Message 68

55. Show as Many Adjustable Bed Bases as Possible 69

56. Sell Unique & Valuable Products 70

Part 3: Will Do Tips 71

57. Always Ask for Testimonials 72

58. Remember "Clean Boots Save Lives" 73

59. Have a Designated Play Area for Kids 74

60. No Solicitations Without Appointment 75

61. Send Thank You Notes to Your Customers 76

62. Survey Your Customers for Important Feedback 77

63. Know What Your Customers are Searching for Online 78

64. Use Google Alerts to Your Advantage 79

65. Build a Marketing Peer Network 80

66. Give Everyone a Story to Behold and Be Told 81

67. Follow and Study Other Local Businesses	82
68. Put Yourself Out There, Don't Hide	83
69. Have an Informational Facebook Page	84
70. Hire Picketers to "Protest" Your Store	85
71. Do Off-Beat Promotions	86
72. Take & Use Photographs	87
73. Have Fun - Host a Contest	88
74. Offer Quality Upgrades & Profit	89
75. Merchandise Your Bedding Accessories	90
76. Uniformity is Important for First Impressions	92
77. Customer Delivery - Do Something With It!	93
Suggested Resources from Jeff Giagnocavo	95
Amplify Your Mattress Sales	96
Renegade Reviews	100
Renegade Mattress Retailer Weekly	101
Test-Drive the Renegade Mattress Retailer Inner Circle	103
The #1 Strategy That Changed It All For Us	105
Automatic Mattress Customers	109
Automatic Mattress Profits	111
My Notes	114

Foreword From Dale T. Read

Those of you who are independent mattress/ bedding retailers must often feel as if you are a combat foot soldier engaged in a heavy, close-range firefight in order to succeed. What with online, bed-in-a-box, the race to the bottom price wars, brand blurring commodity products, and the negative attitude many consumers have about shopping for a mattress, it really must seem like open warfare to win the day by running a successful mattress store.

Every combat veteran knows that there are a couple of things that really make a difference between winning or losing a war. One is having overwhelming firepower with adequate ammunition. The other is fellow soldiers in the trenches with you fighting for each other, covering each other's back.

Jeff Giagnocavo's book offers you an amazing amount of extensive retail marketing fire power spelled out in an easy-to-read, common sense form from a longtime veteran of the mattress retail trenches. Jeff knows what you as an independent store owner or manager are going through.

He is a fellow warrior who offers you concrete idea after idea on marketing, on business planning, on store management, on sales, on how to work with customers, on pricing strategy, on direct marketing, and on wise use of your advertising and marketing dollar. Jeff even addresses the larger issues such as the difference between working "at your business" to grow and differentiate your store and the day-to-day less productive "working in your business."

He talks about guarding against being pulled away from what is really important for your growth and profitability by what appears to be immediate or urgent activities. Jeff talks real life common sense for store owners, and how to make your store brand and your business attractive to consumers. He shares about how to build a reputation that draws in, and keeps mattress consumers coming back. Jeff talks about having a larger mission for your store and really providing superior, quality sleep products for your customers.

This book truly is a handy tool for the busy independent mattress retailer, especially those of you who do not have a lot of free time. The book offers you 77 enumerated and easy-to-follow concrete ideas. To further simplify and organize these high-impact ideas, Jeff has broken the book into three overall parts:

- **Must Do Tips**
- **Should Do Tips**
- **Will Do Tips**

If you are serious about wanting to break away from the mattress retail crowd and really differentiate your store, then this book should become your trusted guide to success at retail.

As the "Association of Manufacturers, Retailers & Suppliers of Specialty Sleep Products", the Specialty Sleep Association (SSA) is committed to learning about and supporting people and programs devoted to building a strong retail mattress marketplace.

As President of the SSA and former Publisher of BEDROOM Magazine (now Sleep Retailer), I first met Jeff Giagnocavo when he spoke at a Furniture Today Bedding Conference a few years ago in Florida. Since then I've followed Jeff at ISPA functions and also recently online at www.RenegadeMattressRetailer.com, *"The PLACE for Independent Mattress Retailers to Discover Expert Advice to Increase Sales."*

We at the SSA believe you simply cannot pack more firepower into 100 pages of practical, hard-hitting suggestions for retailers looking for answers. This book is an invaluable creative marketing and management tool for today's hard-fighting independent mattress and bedding retailer.

Dale T. Read

President of The Specialty Sleep Association (SSA)

The Future of Sleep™

daler@marketingarmgroup.com

www.sleepinformation.org

www.bedfax.org

Ben McClure, Jeff Giagnocavo and Mike Capuzzi

Introduction

We have dropped into your lap 77 things that likely you didn't know you needed to be doing to thrive in today's economy. Therefore, we have made this more of a working tool than theory. This book is meant to be marked up, dog eared, and ragged by the time you are finished.

There are three sections for you to study and implement:

- **Must Do Tips**
- **Should Do Tips**
- **Will Do Tips**

The Must Do Tips section contains things that simply must be done in order to differentiate yourself and thrive in today's economy. They are not meant to be taken lightly or discounted as "that won't work in my business." Trust us, they will work in any business, including yours.

The Should Do Tips section contains action points that aren't mandatory, but certainly are worthy of your time and consideration. Not critical to success, but will no doubt improve your bottom line.

The Will Do Tips section we put together as a listing of quick nuggets, things you should be able to do rather quickly and see positive results on.

It is likely that as you go through this book you will read things that are contradictory to what are our industry norms. We make no apologies for this. Our business, Gardner's Mattress & More, is the anti-mattress store. We are marketers of our business that happen to deliver mattresses.

Our average ticket is 4x the national average, and we have a mechanism in our store that ensures us a 100% closing ratio. We have been featured in SUCCESS Magazine, Fox New Business, Sleep Savvy, and countless other publications. We are changing the way mattresses are sold.

We are against selling on brand, price, and warranties. Everything most everyone else does, we run away from. In a nutshell, most observers in our industry would say we are crazy, but those outside the industry are impressed with all we do to drive our business forward.

This book is an easy read and an actionable guide to help you get in the right mindset that it's not mattresses you sell, rather a good night's sleep. And for most, a good night's sleep is priceless.

Yet, as an industry we promote "buy it today gone tomorrow" $399 queen sets in EVERY single ad. Counterproductive to say the least, at least for us.

If you are tired of competing on price, tired of being stacked up against your competition, just plain tired of playing the games, read on.

Or, if what we have said sent shivers down your spine and will cause you to lose sleep at night, throw this book in the nearest trash can – we cannot help you.

All that is required in reading this book is an open mind that things can be different and your world does not revolve around price only.

It is our sincerest hope that you are able to take action on each of these chapters. But frankly, if you take action on just a few you will be more than happy with the results.

As we have learned, an idea without implementation has no value. So read the book, dog ear some pages of items you like, and then pick one. Implement it. Come back and do another one.

You will find that getting things done yields great reward and soon enough you will have worked through the entire book.

Remember, no business is that much different than the next and when you consider that this book was written by independent mattress retailers, for independent mattress retailers, the information contained within is extremely valuable.

On behalf of my business partners, Ben McClure and Mike Capuzzi, we appreciate the opportunity to bring these money-making tips to you.

Jeff Giagnocavo

Co-Owner, Gardner's Mattress & More

Co-Founder, Renegade Mattress Retailer Inner Circle

Download Examples
Shown Throughout This Book

As a special bonus gift, I will send you various examples shown throughout this book so you can study them and use them to generate ideas for your store.

To download these examples, go to:

www.RenegadeMattressRetailer.com/bonuses

Ben McClure, Dan Kennedy and Jeff Giagnocavo

A Few Words From Dan Kennedy

By name or face alone, you would never know who Dan Kennedy is. However, it is highly likely you have seen or read an ad or bought something as a result of his work with some of America's largest companies. From Guthy Renker (infomercial producers of Procativ®), to Avon and Weight Watchers, Dan Kennedy is the foremost expert in direct response marketing today. We, as owners of Gardner's Mattress & More in Lancaster PA, are privileged to call Dan a customer.

We share this not to impress you but rather to stress that we practice what we preach. As a consumer Dan can, and will travel to most any state or location to purchase something he wants, and it is only by private jet when appropriate. With this in mind we submit his unequivocal recommendation of us and our store:

"I am a harsh critic of most retail stores, restaurants, services and rarely find opportunities to praise anyone who is consistent from the start of a process involving solving my need or problems through getting my money to delivery and fulfillment and after-care. Many get part of it right, few get it all right. Disney does. But, just as example, recently, Fleming's, a very pricey steakhouse, no. And it seems it can't necessarily be bought. This past year, 3-Day Blinds got a 100% score from my wife and I. A much higher priced door company you'd expect excellence from, a 20% score. I am picky.

I travel to a different state than I reside to go to my dentist, even for regular hygiene. I was certainly willing to fly to Lancaster to finally get a mattress that would give me a good night's sleep without a stiff, aching back in the morning.

Knowing of your store well in advance of stepping forward as a customer, as an example of exceptional marketing which I have featured in my book and newsletter read by tens of thousands of business owners, I had high expectations – but still, I hold my breath waiting for the train to veer off-track every time I buy something.

So, Carla and I had an absolutely perfect experience. You and your folks are expert, knowledgeable, and efficient. The Dream Room experience works as advertised – it is far superior to the traditional pushing hand down on and lying down on a mattress for a few minutes, next, next, and next. Every detail of product, sale and delivery was attended to as promised. The slight delay with importing the bed for valid reasons communicated and well managed.

What I would say most to others is that there is a different experience waiting for them with you than they will have anywhere else. It is respectful. And you have a diagnostic and experimental process so that the customer winds up with the best bed for them. This is the essence of top-level selling; when the process serves the merchant or provider but also authentically serves the best interests of the customer. My recommendation is unequivocal."

~ **Dan S. Kennedy, Marketing Strategist & Author**

Download an Interview With Dan Kennedy on How to Attract Affluent Mattress Buyers

To get a copy of a special interview I did with the legendary Dan Kennedy, go to:

www.RenegadeMattressRetailer.com/bonuses

Part 1
Must Do Tips

1. Realize You Have Five Types of People In Your Business

One of the most profound things you can do to reinvent your mattress retail business and boost sales is also one of the easiest things you can do, since all it requires initially is a broadening of the way you look at your business.

If I asked 100 independent mattress retailers the question, "What is the biggest problem you have in your business?" I believe 97 of them would say, "I don't have enough customers."

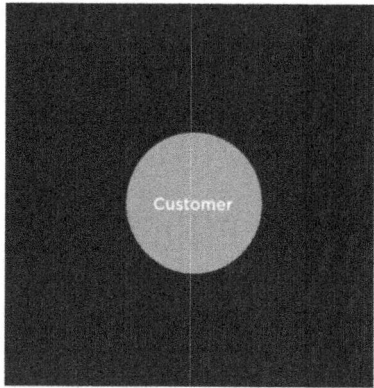

It's like a knee-jerk reaction to only focus on "the customer", and when you talk to retailers they tend to incorrectly label every person who "flows" through their business as a "customer."

However, as I am about to show you, this is narrow-sighted and limits your ability to make the amount of money you want to make.

After studying the most successful businesses in the world, I quickly realized in order to capitalize on all the opportunities in my stores each day, I needed to broaden my view of how people interact and flow through my business.

The result is that my mattress retail business and YOUR mattress retail business actually has five different types of people who are interacting in it on any given day.

These five types of people are **Leads, Prospects, Customers, Fans and Friends**.

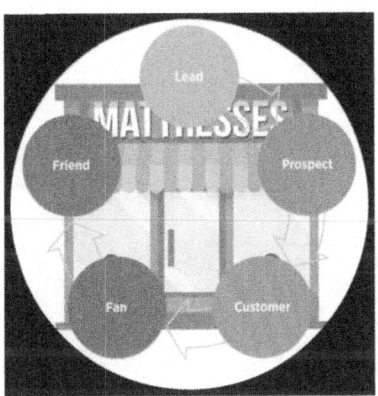

- Leads are individuals who have responded to your marketing, typically making an information exchange with your business (their contact info for your educational info) but have yet to visit, or have an in-depth phone call with you or your staff.
- Prospects are Leads who have visited your store but have yet to make a purchase.
- Customers are Prospects who have made a purchase.
- Fans are Customers who refer, review and/or give a testimonial.
- Friends are Leads, Prospects, Customers and Fans who we are staying in touch with over months or possibly years with the intention of moving them forward to getting them to make a repeat purchase. It's not their job to remember us. It is our job to remember them.

When you look at your mattress retail business through this wider lens, you realize you have five unique audiences you can be marketing to at any given point in time. You also realize that each type of person offers unique profit opportunities that aren't tapped when you only think in terms of just "customers." It's important you understand this concept and what it means to the future of your business.

2. Your Job is Not Selling Mattresses, It's Marketing

You've seen it before. Your favorite local eatery goes out of business. Why? Well it's not because the food wasn't good or that the business owner didn't try hard, it is simply because he was too caught up in the "doing" and not the "marketing" of the business.

Answering the phones, putting out the fires, being at the beck and call of every little distraction, it's easy to lose sight of what really needs to be done as a business owner.

Your primary focus is to steer the ship. Be the captain, be the Marketer of your business.

Just like you should have a business plan in place you should have a marketing plan, budget, and a calendar for marketing. For us, I contend that we have a head start on most other businesses as we have major promotional periods and often manufacturer sponsored events to get the ball rolling.

However, when you focus solely on the holidays that everyone else is talking about too, is that really a solid plan or does it make sense to develop your own calendar of events and promotions? Having your own calendar of events, promotions, and touch points with your own customer list is simply one of the most powerful things you can do to secure your own success.

When you properly market to your own list you can offer promotions and specials that your competition simply will not, cannot, or are even aware that you are offering. Float like a butter fly and sting like a bee. Get busy "marketing" and you will profit, while they are too busy "doing".

3. Always Be Marketing (A.B.M.)

Sadly, many business owners and not just mattress store owners, simply take the field of dreams approach to business. "If I'm open for business, they will buy from me."

This couldn't be farther from the truth. And no, your price match guarantee won't do much either, everyone has one of those. You need to do more marketing. You need to promote yourself more. You're in the "marketing of a mattress store business" and in order to rise above the competition and succeed, you must never forget this truth and must always be marketing.

You need to keep your marketing radar on 24-7 and look for opportunities to communicate more effectively with prospects and customers. Always be asking yourself questions like,

What's happening in the news or current events which I can leverage in my marketing?

Is there a special holiday or event coming up which allows me to create a unique marketing message?

Along with this, every marketing piece you produce should have these four essential elements:

1. An attention grabbing headline
2. An offer
3. A call-to-action
4. A deadline

When you're in A.B.M. mode, you'll see opportunities all around you, which will allow you to offer greater value to your customers and prospects.

4. Evaluate and Monitor Every Marketing Effort

Three letters that changed our life: R. O. I. otherwise known as Return On Investment.

If it can't be measured by the dollars generated, it is not worth doing. We've always known that we didn't have the big Madison Ave ad budget, but up until a few years ago we thought that was the only way to market any business. Then we had the light bulb moment. All we were doing in our advertising was putting money in our advertiser's pockets.

Brand awareness, impressions, reputation building, likes, and followers = BULLSHIT

Money Spent versus Money In The Bank = ROI. Trackable sales, through trackable mediums. When you place a newspaper ad, have an offer unique in that ad along with a unique tracking phone number for the ad.

Have a contest on Facebook? Fine, but make it unique to Facebook. Print a newsletter and have a unique offer in there, along with a tracking phone number printed just for the newsletter.

Every advertising medium works for us. If it doesn't produce a minimum an ROI of 10:1, it won't be around long. A 10:1 ROI means that you have, at minimum, kept advertising expenses at 10% comparative to sales.

This means for every $1 we spend we simply must generate, in sales, a minimum of $10 for each dollar spent. Now, I know this is counter-productive to what everyone in the industry will tell you but I challenge you to consider just how much of their branding and awareness actually translates into money in your bank account?

5. Have a Unique Selling Position

A unique selling position lets your customers know immediately why they should do business with you instead of all the other places they can buy a mattress from. Your unique selling position (USP) is UNIQUE to you. This is not about you. It is about why your customer should choose to buy a mattress from you and you alone. How you can help them and why you are the one and only place to spend their hard earned money with.

Your USP must always answer the question, "*What's in it for me?*"

Keep in mind that in today's economy, it is not the latest and greatest electronic gizmo and gadget dollars competing for the customer; rather it is everything else, including doing NOTHING.

That's right, nothing. Given the heartbeat of today's economy, sadly our customer is choosing to delay their new mattress purchase and doing nothing.

Our USP at Gardner's Mattress & More is that we help our customers understand exactly how we can help them sleep better at night. Here it is:

At Gardner's we help you wake up happy. Sleep is powerful and a new sleep system from Gardner's helps you be a better you. Our process to find the perfect mattress is guaranteed with our **120 Night Wake Up Happy Comfort Promise**. If you're not the best you after sleeping on a Gardner's Mattress & More sleep system we will happily exchange it with absolutely no fee to you.

Think about your own USP and why your customer should do business with you out of all the other choices they have.

6. Clearly Define Your Mission

Much like your USP or unique selling position, this can't be the same old bland mission statement. This should be who your company is and what it stands for. Compare our mission to our USP. Your mission should be a battle cry or rally call for your team. If they can execute on your mission statements in every customer interaction, phone call, delivery and sales presentation you will easily live your mission and bring your USP to life.

Here's ours at Gardner's:

Purpose: Improve the lives of others through a better night's sleep.

Values:

- You before us.
- Say what we'll do and do what we say.
- Demand excellence in all that we do.

Mission:

- Move from success to significance.

Inspirational Quote:

- "Integrity is what you do when no one else is looking."

7. Have a System for Everything

This is about as broad of a topic in this book and there's too much to talk about it in one small chapter. It should go without saying that you need to systematize your business if you'd like to grow, have more freedom within your business, or sell your business. A business without systems runs in constant chaos, sucks up all of your personal time, and leaves your business with no value when it comes time to sell it.

Some aspects of your business in need of systems include:

- Point-of-sale sales tracking and reporting
- Customer management and communication
- Sales choreography and scripting
- Store policies
- Employee job descriptions, expectations, and guidelines
- Delivery procedures

Systems typically require some blood, sweat, and tears to create, enforce, and implement. However, we have made it very easy for mattress retailers to implement a proven suite of advertising, marketing and sales systems.

To See a Neat Video On How We Use Automated Systems Watch This Video:

https://youtu.be/DYhWMf814VM

---

8. Develop a Sales Process & Choreography

We have all been there. A slow day, the phones are dead, and you have checked the door three times to make sure it isn't locked. Nothing is happening. Then it happens - it's 6:35 PM and in walks a customer. It's important to get out of the starting blocks properly, but since you have not seen a customer all day you're not feeling sharp or on point.

Of course, I'm not talking about the usual greeting of "Hi my name is Jeff, what brings you into our store?" I'm talking about real choreography that gets the customer engaged with you from the first time you open your mouth.

Remember, customers view purchasing a mattress as a "need" item not a "want" item. They put us right up there with car tires. Few, if any, wake up in the morning and say "I really want to go purchase a new mattress today." Those statements are usually reserved for electronics, cars, & jewelry, among many other items our customer can choose to spend their money on.

Customers have come to view a mattress purchase as a task, and something they have to gear up for and do battle with us over. It turns into a pissing contest between all the stores they will go to in the hopes that they will win. However, I have often found that the net result of a pissing contest is that both parties, customer included, end up yellow and wet.

Our sales choreography centers around education and pushing the relief button on the pressure cooker that is mattress shopping. We deliver real value and real information that is helpful whether they buy from us or not. We often have customers come back after experiencing our competition and apologize to us that they even considered anyone else.

9. Educate Your Customers as to the Value You Offer

Here is where our industry does not perform so well. Value does not mean a guaranteed low price with a two point font paragraph of weasel clause behind it.

Value is what the customer gets, or in other words, the benefit of doing business with you.

- *How do you help them?*
- *How do they benefit?*
- *What's in it for them?*

You will notice the above three questions are a belief and mindset shift throughout this book. Our value statement is: We help people wake up happy and pain free.

Break down this value statement and you have a person that is no longer waking up with aches and pains feeling more tired than when they went to bed. Their back is not stiff and they don't have to take a few minutes to get out of bed.

They are happy, not grumpy or in a bad mood because yet again, they wake up sore, tired, stiff and unrested. This is true value and you must educate your customers about it.

10. Understand Your #1 Product is YOU!

Over the years, you've likely had many brands on your floor come and go. And truth be told, when a customer comes into your store, they see a sea of white and beige rectangles. This reality begs a different approach to how you position yourself.

Often when we are away from the store for a few days, the customers that come in and ask for us by name can hardly believe that we are not working. This is ok though if you have the right staff. We market ourselves. We put our personality into the business and we differentiate ourselves this way.

Throughout this book you will read of many different ways to differentiate your business from others. But remember, it is you that your customers are buying. Get them to know you, like you, and trust you and the money will follow. It is a very simple formula.

It is hard to like and trust a logo. It's even harder to trust a big corporate brand in this day and age. But let your customers get to know YOU, do things that will make them like YOU, and ultimately, they will trust YOU. In the end, they give YOU the business.

11. Build Your #1 Asset Your List

There is money in a list. Don't believe me? Simply look to the list broker industry, or better yet, Publishers Clearing House. You really don't think they just collect names and hand out millions in cash prizes do you? No. They build a list, survey the list, and then sell the list to other businesses.

Well guess what? There is no need to ever buy a list again. You can build your own list of customers.

Develop a system to effectively capture and retain all the customer addresses you sell to. All too often, many mattress store owners look to the newest thing they can do to acquire new customers. In actuality, there is money in the list you already have paid for.

Use it more than once, and remember most people have a need for more than just one mattress. And it's likely that you have done a good job so there are many reasons to go back to your existing customers for referrals, special events, testimonials, special offers on alternate items like accessories, and even additional purchases.

A good list of active and engaged clients will be your most valuable asset over the life of your business.

12. Always Capture Name and Email

First, if you aren't offering a downloadable item from your website, like our proven mattress buying guides that are part of **Automatic Mattress Customers** (see page 105 for more details) or a "bring-it-into-the-store" coupon, voucher or offer of some kind, do it. But here's the key – you need to know who requests the item. This information is very valuable. First, it's highly likely that this customer will be in your store very soon, so you can alert your staff to properly welcome the customer.

But what if that customer doesn't come in? With the proper CRM (customer relationship management) software, you can communicate with this lead and get them to visit. You can track the effectiveness of your different offers by knowing how many downloads and conversions you get.

13. Always Follow-up With Everybody!

Today more than ever in the world of tweets, status updates, and technology overload, we as a society are attention challenged. So if you don't make a sale today, be sure to follow-up tomorrow. Of course, you need to have the contact information to do so but today's customer likes to know you are interested in them and that you would like to earn their business.

We all like to feel wanted and appreciated and a simple phone call or email goes a very long way.

Try this:

"Thank you for the time yesterday and if you have any additional feedback for me at the moment, I would love to hear it."

Compare that statement with this one, "Hi, I'm Joe from Joe's Mattress, I'm just checking in."

What exactly is Joe checking into? A hotel? When you ask for feedback, it requires more than a "Yes" or "No" answer and immediately dissolves any pressure a customer may feel.

Our Automatic Mattress Customer solution for independent mattress retailers follow-up with people who have expressed a real interest in buying a quality mattress—automatically.

24 hours a day, 7 days a week.

For more details about Automatic Mattress Customers, see page 105.

14. Always Ask for a Response & Provide a Way to Respond

How many ads have you run over the years with a manufacturer's drop in, a price, and your phone #? Hundreds? Maybe even thousands? How many of your ads that you run today have a reason to respond now or even a deadline?

The issue we have with most mattress store advertising today is that it only helps the people looking to buy a mattress now. Not next week, two weeks from now or even a month from now. The issue with how most advertise today is that it is for today's customers only, not for the future ones. Think about this - what are you doing now for the customer that is considering a new mattress purchase? It's been a while but their bed is ok. Maybe some aches and pains show up every once and a while but they just aren't in the market right now.

If you are honest with yourself, you are doing nothing. Nothing at all. Your advertising only provides a solution for the customer in the market today who is ready to buy now. A free report, a book or a recorded information piece is a great reason to respond now. No, they are not buying today and that's ok, but you are beginning to show you are the store with answers to questions they have, or better yet question they didn't even know they should be asking.

Always put into your ads reasons to respond – frankly, this could be as simple as a coupon download or special offer code in exchange for a name and email. Or it could be something as robust as a mattress buying guide. Either way, give your customer a reason to start the buying process with you and you alone.

15. Always Have an Offer & Deadline

As an industry, we are pretty good at this one. The problem is, there is always a sale and as soon one ends another one begins. The customer knows this and frankly scoffs at our attempt to create any sort of urgency.

But in the event you are not including a deadline currently in your ads, do this now. We find it best to go 10-14 days. A deadline creates urgency; no deadline means your prospect can wait, so why should they act now? There is no reason too. That twin mattress will be there in a month for $99, so why get it now when Grandma is only coming in two months anyway; we will go when we need it.

But if you were to run an ad that created urgency via a deadline or scarcity by limiting quantity or number of sets allowed to be sold at this price, that is something people will get off their butts for.

16. Offer a Rock-Solid Guarantee

Most of your competitors offer a guarantee such as a comfort exchange, but that's not the reason for you to have one. Your competitor's guarantees are there to protect against poor salesmanship. Your guarantees are in place to protect your customer's investment. There's a difference.

Your competition uses a guarantee as a "buy it now" closer, meaning that their sales associate has not done a thorough job with the customer. Your guarantees will be in place because your prospect has been through your process to fit the customer to the mattress that best fits their unique sleep needs. The guarantee must be clearly written and should be offered to every customer that qualifies. See the Gardner's Guarantee at:

www.GardnersMattressAndMore.com/Guarantee

17. Fire Yourself

Have you ever been to a McDonald's where you actually see the owner? The only acknowledgement that your local McDonalds is owned by someone is the plaque hanging on the wall. Ever wonder why that is?

Systems and proper business management.

What you should know and understand is that the sooner you let go of the $10 hour an work, you can focus on the $100 an hour work. Accomplish this and you will find there are many hours in a day available to really work on your business instead of in your business.

Let me repeat that - work ON your business, not IN your business.

True entrepreneurs understand that their primary function is to drive the business forward, and in most cases that means your sole focus should be on marketing your mattress store.

This is your goal; this focus of being the driving force behind marketing your business is what will ensure your success.

18. Stop Being Your Own Assistant

In the movie "Office Space," one of my favorite lines from Ron Livingston's character is: *"I guess in any given day I really only do about 15 minutes of actual work here."*

Funny when you're a rank and file employee, not so funny when you own the business.

So how many hours are you really working? And of those hours, how many are dedicated to tasks that you could pay someone to do for you and free you up to actually work ON your business?

One of the best moves we made was promoting one of our long time employees from lead delivery driver to internal operations and salesman. His primary function is making sure all the paperwork is done, orders are placed, deliveries are scheduled, service issues handled, and basically does anything we shouldn't be doing, or no longer wish to do.

Every day we focus on marketing our business. And you should too.

What did this personal shift cost us? About $600 a week in increased payroll. (We did have to hire a new delivery person to fill the vacancy) What has it meant to us so far? About a 10% increase in business! So to cover this new investment in our business, all we needed to do is sell 3 extra $500 sets a week, and keep in mind our average ticket is $2700 - so not too hard to do.

And as a side note, our delivery man turned operations manager and now salesman is writing business at the highest margin in the store!

19. Hire Eagles, Not Turkeys!

This is pretty simple, but so many get it wrong and put up with poor quality people for far too long. Order takers will kill you. You know the type, those people that are happy to let the customer lead them around their store by the nose and push them around into what they want. Eagles soar, turkeys don't. Eagles are graceful and high flying, turkeys waddle.

Now don't get me wrong, what we do here at Gardner's Mattress & More is extremely customer focused, but it will be done in our format and to our choreography. In the end, this is beneficial to both the customer and us.

I know it's easy to say to yourself - I can't possibly let go of "Jim." He's been with me for 15 years and has a family. Well guess what, you owe it to yourself and to Jim and his family, to get Jim to soar high or cut him loose. He's not doing you or himself any favors. While you have let him waddle on for the last 5 years instead of having him soar, he has cost you untold tens of thousands and piled on even more stress and debt personally.

You must challenge your employees always to be the eagle to achieve new heights in their career and sales numbers. We do this by constantly watching the numbers. More than sales volume, we monitor closing percentage, adjustable bed attachment, pillow sales, mattress protectors sold, and margin on each and every item.

We reward eagle behavior with bonuses and time off. Too much turkey behavior is rewarded with....well you get the point.

20. Have a Website That Engages Your Customer

Study our site: **www.GardnersMattressAndMore.com.**

It is very different than what you might be accustomed to in the mattress industry. There is a clear direction of what we want the customer to do, and that is to get our book. No "in your face, this weekend only, super-duper special." Rather, what we want the customer to do is front and center - get our book via email.

You get what you ask for in life, right? So why not ask for what we know creates the best customer for us, an educated customer with our book in hand. Second, our website works as a consumer education device. Since we know, and you should too, that all customers really view a mattress as just a white rectangle at first, we take the position to educate them about how to transform that white rectangle into a sleep system that is fit to their specific sleep needs.

21. Use Video to Direct Traffic and Increase Opt-Ins

Forget about whether or not you are good on camera. There is enormous power of what a simple video can do for your website, so you must give it a try. A great use of a video is to direct your website lead to do what it is that you want them to do.

If you have an opt-in box on your home page that you want them to fill out, put a 30 second video next to the box welcoming them to the site, and directing them to fill out the form. You'll be pleased to see your opt-in rate quadruple. All you need is a decent camera with video recording capability and a web guy who can put it on your site for you. You could record it today and have it on your site converting for you tomorrow.

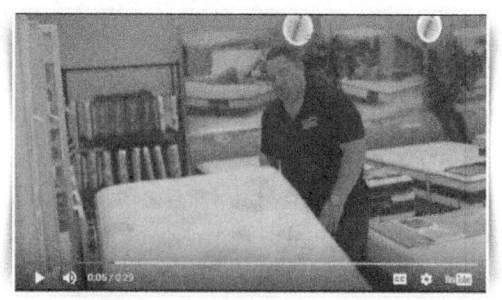

22. Raise Your Prices & Profit

Too often, the lowest price is associated with the lowest quality. Why do you want the "price only" shoppers that drive you nuts? Only morons think they're getting something for nothing. I agree your prices need to be competitive, but when you offer unique and superior products to your competitors, you can charge more for them.

Also, when your customers look to you, the bedding experts, for advice and their goal is truly a better night's sleep, they will invest more with you. When you position yourself properly, price is much less of a concern.

To do this you simply must raise the level of perceived value higher than the price asked. When the value of what you are selling exceeds the price you are requesting you are no longer selling, you are affirming that the sleep solution presented is the only choice for the customer to have.

There are various tips in this book to help you build value in your sales presentations - in the eye of the customer in front of you. Make sure you check tip 52.

23. Address the "Payment Elephant" in the Room

Gone are the days of simply asking *"Will that be cash or check?"*

Did you know that 30% of our country is comprised of people who have poor to no credit and struggle to use any other kind of financial vehicle other than payments? Traditionally when it comes to buying furniture and mattresses this demographic purchases form rent to own stores. Over the last decade the advent of No Credit Check Financing has brought these customers into traditional stores and away from credit houses and rent to own.

The key here is for you to understand and learn which customer you have in front of you. A touchy subject to say the least, we've been told since our grade school years to not discuss money. But you simply must in order to maximize sales.

I've found it's best to understand early how the customer intends to invest in their new sleep set. You can ask *"Tell me, would you be open to no interest financing that keeps your money in your pocket over the long term and is free to you?"* This simple question can quickly cut through the payment fog and better frame your presentation and subsequent offers.

Recently, as we added no credit check financing to our payment options, we can also ask, *"Will you be paying with cash, check, credit card or would you like to use our take it home today layaway?"*

Understanding the types of buyers and their wallet while being focused on the language you use to understand how you'll be paid will help you close more sales and craft a better presentation while maximizing bottom line profits.

24. Always Ask For Referrals

Referrals and word of mouth advertising are simply the best types of advertising any business owner can ask for. A glowing endorsement from a happy customer simply cannot be matched with any other advertising medium.

But like testimonials, it must be part of a system and something that is done automatically with each and every sale.

We have chosen, upon delivery, to leave behind a referral form for our customer to fill out. We collect name and address, and subsequently have a system to mail the referral a package of our materials - who we are and how we can help them sleep better.

In the online world, we do this via email, and within our CRM system we have a customized referral sequence that once we mark the customer delivered, a referral sequence begins in which customers can refer us with just a few simple clicks. In both cases, when the customer completes our referral form in it's entirety we offer them a $20 gift card to their choice of store - Amazon, iTunes, Dunkin Donuts or Starbucks.

Note: Giving customers an option to pick a reward will raise your referral rate because they can now pick their reward as opposed to being told what it is, and they may not like it.

Download a Copy of Our Referral Form

To download a copy of the referral form we use, go to:

www.RenegadeMattressRetailer.com/bonuses

25. Negotiate Ad Rates on Your Terms

If you advertise in your local newspaper, you already know that newspaper rates are ridiculous. But you also know that newspaper advertising, when done properly, can be very effective. If you're like us, and we think you are, you don't have it in your budget to be in the newspaper as much as your competition. This means you must be razor sharp in negotiating you ad rates.

Typically, ad rates will vary depending on how much ad space you buy during a calendar year. The more you advertise, the lower the rate. What you need to do is determine the size of ad you need and how many of those ads you want to run in a particular time period. Then determine the available budget you have for newspaper advertising. The key is letting them know that you'll run XX amount of ads over the next 6 or 12 months as they'll want to see your commitment as opposed to running an ad here and there.

Go to your rep with that plan and let them know that you'll advertise in the paper if they can meet your requirements. If they cannot, let them nicely know that you won't be a partner in their advertising. It's likely that you won't get them to agree to your first proposal, but you'll get a better than advertised rate. It doesn't hurt to try does it?

26. Host an Anniversary Event

Every business has a built-in reason for a profitable event and you've got to take advantage of it. Find an important event in your business history and highlight it. The easiest is the anniversary of your store opening, but it could also be based around a location change or ownership change. And here's a tip – plan your event during a non-peak sales period.

For example, if your event falls three weeks before Memorial Day, wait until after. It's likely that you'll get increased traffic during that holiday anyway. A better time to run it is in the historically poor traffic month of June, after the Memorial Day rush. Make your event fun by running a contest or hosting a customer appreciation event at your store where you invite your best customers...and tell them to bring a friend!

27. Make it Right

Not only is this good business advice, it's good advice to live by. If a customer raises a concern, they should not be viewed as a "problem" or a "pain-in-the-you-know-what." Often, when a concern arises, it's a result of a broken system. This is an opportunity to not only make your customer happy, but to fix your broken system. Thank the customer for bringing it to your attention.

Work quickly to resolve the customer's concern and communicate with them every step of the process. They'll rave about your service. However, if you delay your service responses or ignore their issues, you're sunk. You'll never regain their trust and you'll never gather a referral from them. This does not mean you give in to your customer if they are being unruly or unreasonable; you've got to stand your ground. But make sure you work to find a quick resolution, but always make it right.

To not make it right risks a negative reputation online and in your community. Every retailer I know has at least one poor review. And yes, there are always two sides to every story. Our negative reviews exist because we either moved away from our core competency, selling premium sleep systems, and sold the customer some furniture we had access to - which we have no business doing. Or they exist because there was a miscommunication on a deeply discounted floor model.

The question you need to ask yourself when it comes time to make it right is this, "What would I pay to make any of my negative reviews go away?" When you're honest with yourself you'll likely realize that the cost of making it right is far less than the number you'd pay to make a bad review disappear. So why not make the customer happy, have the ability to get a positive review from them and maintain a terrific reputation?

Part 2:
Should Do Tips

28. Use a CRM System

CRM stands for Customer Relationship Management. There are many solutions out there. So many in fact, we're not going to list them here, simply google CRM. It is very important to not let the customers who have come in your door but don't buy, leave without getting their information.

A good CRM does everything for you automatically once you enter the information. For example, you can immediately send them everything you would want your customer to know about their forthcoming mattress purchase.

I submit to you that when customers don't buy, an exchange has still been made. They have, hopefully, learned something about their mattress set they will purchase and you have taken the time to educate them. The exchange of time has been made. When you give good information and have well thought out sales choreography, as referenced in this book, you should be comfortable enough to ask for contact information. We do this all the time and rarely, if ever, fail to collect full name, address, phone number, and email.

Imagine what you could do to follow-up with each customer that has been given a presentation and not bought with all their contact information. Now imagine if it was all done for you automatically.

29. Create and Maintain a Marketing Calendar

This is simply one of your best assets you can acquire for your business. Some companies have a business plan, even fewer have a marketing plan.

When we applied for our SBA Loan, we had a business plan and a marketing plan for each bank we met with. It was no surprise that the bank that was most impressed with the marketing plan we prepared decided to lend us the money. They knew we were serious and had a plan on HOW to acquire customers, not just a plan to spend the money we were asking for.

Don't think a marketing plan will help you? Before we even opened our doors, our marketing plan enabled us to get SBA funding in the first quarter of 2011, when business lending was at an all-time low and it only took 98 days to get our funds wired into our account.

But that's not the real reason why you should have one, just a magnified example. The real reason is it keeps you focused. Focused on what you should be doing between President's Day, Memorial Day, 4th of July, and Labor Day. How many times have you said to yourself, holy crap - we need more business? And typically the answer is to put more ads in the paper, do a coupon type ad, or call up the radio station. That is all very reactionary and adds little real value to your business.

A solid marketing plan adds real equity to your business. You lay out what you feel will work, implement it, track it, and measure it. You cut what doesn't work and keep what does. Next year you go back and fill in the failures. Soon enough, you have a real plan to use year after year that you can build on. Oh, and the peace-of-mind in this valuable business tool isn't too bad either.

30. Create Your Own Marketing Library

Ever see something in the mail that was really cool?

Ever open an email because the subject line caught your attention?

What did you do with these things? Toss them? That's ok. But from this day forward, please do yourself a favor and keep these items. Put that mail in a file folder, and print those emails out too.

What you are creating is your own marketing library. The best marketers know that a good offer, a good headline, and a good guarantee can be used in most any business.

Begin to create this library of great marketing examples. I came to understand long ago that it is far easier to get inspiration from things that work than it is to create something with no history of successful conversion.

If you see a business in your local market place that is widely successful and they continuously extend the same special, offer, or guarantee, get their marketing materials and study them.

Keep mail and print emails that catch your attention. Start assembling your own marketing library and you will find inspiration is right at your fingertips.

31. Test New Marketing Ideas Frequently

Don't be afraid to innovate, create, and implement new marketing ideas and concepts! Seriously, some of the best ideas sound crazy at first, but if you don't try, how will you ever be unique? There is a caveat though – you must test and measure each new idea to know if it is something you keep doing or scrap. If you have trouble coming up with your own ideas, start compiling a library of neat things you see other advertisers do in other industries and apply it to your business.

I can't say that everything we've tried has been a success and no question, that's frustrating. But the enormous success we've had with some of our best ideas more than make up for some trial and error.

Download a List of Marketing Media Ideas

To get a copy of a list of marketing media we use in our stores, go to:

www.RenegadeMattressRetailer.com/bonuses

---

32. Resurrect Promotions from the Past

If it ain't broke don't fix it, right?

This applies to marketing mattresses, for sure. Obviously, you cannot run the same promotion or offer all the time, but if you find something that works, determine the best times of the year to run it and go with it!

For example, we know that a Free box spring promotion works for our business around the big holidays – President's Day, Memorial Day, and Labor Day. We may not run it each holiday, but we know it's proven to get good results. We know that running a "support local business" type of ad with a charitable component works great around Black Friday and Small Business Saturday. We are constantly trying new things in our ads, but we maintain a library of past successful promotions that we reference and steal from often. Create your library and reference it often.

33. Publish a Customer Newsletter

A monthly or bi-monthly newsletter is a great way to keep in touch with your customers, let them know what is going on with you and your business, and keep them interacting with you. Perhaps you'd run a contest in your newsletter, or offer a special gift if they visit and check out one of your new products. You customers will love hearing about your new dog or milestone your child just passed. Don't be shy, tell them what is going on with you and your staff. After the first one, they'll be excited to see the next one and learn what is going on within your business.

On the surface, publishing a newsletter sounds like a daunting task. Where will I get the content each month, who will design it, and how in the world can I get it printed and mailed without blowing the budget? Thankfully, there are great newsletter services out there that are easy to use and cost effective. There are even some with online templates where you log in, pick from pre-done templates, enter some of your own content, enter your credit card and boom, you're done.

Another newsletter idea is to involve complimentary (to what you sell) local businesses and actually get them to pay you to be in your newsletter. If your newsletter is going out to your best 1,000 customers, don't you think that is pretty valuable to another business? It's likely that you can recoup your newsletter investment with that little nugget right there.

34. Create & Give WOW! Packages

WOW! packages are unexpected gifts we give the different audiences in our business (e.g. customers, referrals, etc.). They are designed to make the recipient go WOW! when they receive it. For example, every new customer who has a mattress delivered gets a fun little WOW! package left on their new mattress.

We include some homemade treats, promotional items and a referral form.

Our customers love this little gift and share this simple, but intentional act, with their friend and family.

Your WOW! packages don't need to be expensive, but they should be intentionally designed to help the person (and make them go WOW!).

35. Use Stories in Your Marketing

Stories are unique, plain and simple. No one else can tell your story, so why not tell it to your audience and stick out from all of your competitors? A story can be something that happened in your business, a customer experience, or something that happened in your personal life that is relevant. Don't be afraid to take some time, write some engaging copy, and use it. Stories work great in advertorials, blog posts, emails delivered via a CRM, and even mailed letters to new leads.

However, don't forget about using stories in "traditional" media like newspapers. We've done ads where three-quarters of the ad is a letter telling a story. Not everyone will take the time to read it, but the ones that do will be easy, higher end sales for you. Your personality should shine through your stories, so keep them light and entertaining. Appropriate humor is always good. People love buying from people they know, like, and trust and stories will do exactly that.

36. Use Giveaways to Attract New Customers

People love free stuff, even if it is something small and especially if it is unannounced. In our marketing to new leads, we will offer the lead a free gift if they visit the store within three weeks of receiving the message. The gift isn't anything spectacular – a large umbrella, travel mug, car wash certificate, or a $5 Starbucks gift card; but you'd be surprised how well it works! First, what other store in your market is going to give them something for free? They'll remember you best, that's for sure. Second, if a free gift helps close a few thousand dollar sale, it's a no-brainer.

We'll also offer a free gift to someone who has visited the store but doesn't make a purchase. Again, a time sensitive, "make your purchase by X date and we'll give you a free gift" type of message works incredibly well.

Another idea is to use other local businesses as your free offers. For example, if you have a local coffee shop near you, go to them and see if you can get them to give you free vouchers that you can give to your customers. The coffee shop gains a new customer and you make someone's day by giving them a free gift.

I mentioned doing an unannounced gift and this is powerful too. On every delivery, we give a gift of two yummy cake pops (if you're not familiar with cake pops, Google them – they're an awesome gift!).

37. Use Testimonials the Right Way

We use testimonials a lot. We call it testimonial marketing and it is highly productive and produces a hefty return on use. The difference between our testimonials and those from our competition is that our testimonials are undeniably AUTHENTIC. Not a single testimonials looks like this:

"The Gardner's guys ROCK, I love my mattress." - John B.

They look like this:

GARDNER'S MAKES PEOPLE HAPPY:

We screen capture Facebook comments, scan handwritten notes, and re-purpose testimonial forms our customers complete.

When we use testimonials, we also make sure that we send a testimonial specific to the product our new customer is considering. So if they are interested in a Tempur-Pedic mattress set, we send them a testimonial specific to Tempur-Pedic. This affirms to the customer that their peers, via the testimonial, enjoy their Tempur-Pedic mattress too.

38. Become A Trusted Advisor, Write A Column

Out of all the media out there, printed material is still by far the most trustworthy medium you can advertise in. Over the years, we have written many articles or advertorials. We often talk about sleep issues, health issues that a new mattress can fix, sleeping hot, our Dream Room, our private consultations or any other topic related to sleep that:

A) our customer will enjoy reading about

B) that relates to something we can offer

There is little sense to take the time to write about a topic that you can't help the reader with. We identify a problem, agitate the problem, and then offer a solution that we can provide.

39. Become a Trusted Authority, Write a Book

Our world-famous mattress buying guide, "**What's Keeping You Up at Night**" is our most valuable marketing asset. It is the cornerstone of all of our online and offline marketing efforts.

This is a consumer education piece and when our customers come in the door with guide in hand, we know we have a customer, not just a prospect, but a customer walking the door.

They are educated about what questions to ask, what problems they need to focus on that are an issue for them, and they know exactly how we operate and what to expect. The stress level is greatly reduced and the trust level is elevated.

Readers are buyers, plain and simple. They have committed time to us by reading the book, and they are invested in us and no one else. If we go back to our statement from earlier in the book about the exchange of time and information, we have given them great information and they have invested time.

With our book in their hands the sale has begun, and all we need to do is affirm we are the right choice, have the right solution, and we write up the sale.

40. Be an Award Winner In Your Community

In most local communities, local publications will run "favorite" or "best of" contests. While on the surface these seem like petty popularity contests, they are crucial to establishing your store as the leader and trusted authority in your market.

For example, Gardner's is a seven-time winner of the Lancaster Newspapers Reader's Choice Award for "Favorite Mattress/Bedding store. We take EVERY opportunity to tell our prospective and current customers this fact. Every ad, every email, our wall behind our sales desk, our delivery truck, and more display this fact. And it doesn't take much to win them. Go to your best customers and ask them to vote for you. It's as easy as that.

LANCASTER'S FAVORITE

MATTRESS STORE

7 YEARS AND COUNTING...

2016 - 2015 - 2014 - 2013 - 2012 - 2011 - 2010

41. Make Your Own Currency

The word "coupon" is too vague and overused. Why not make up your own sales currency? At Gardner's, we have "Ben Bucks." Ben Bucks are special printed vouchers that resemble real money that allow the customer a discount of purchases over certain amounts. We also get creative with the $ amounts which are more effective than the standard $25 or $50 off coupons.

We give Ben Bucks to leads that visit the store but do not buy, and we allow Ben Bucks to be downloaded online. Of course, we capture name and email with every coupon download so we know exactly who downloaded them. We also can communicate quickly with that lead as they are likely to make a bedding buying decision soon.

Good for $97 off a purchase of $950 or more!

excludes Tempur Pedic and iComfort

Not valid on prior purchases, and cannot be combined with other offers/coupons.

42. Have Fun – Turn Yourself into a Cartoon

While a cartoon or caricature may not be applicable everywhere (for example, I'd put a real picture of you with your guarantee), they're a fun way to brand yourself and your store, while getting away with saying some things that you might not otherwise say. You simply can get away with more when you're a cartoon.

Change your caricature's look with each holiday (think Christmas, Thanksgiving, St. Patrick's Day, etc.). Run a contest with your character where the first people to find them in your ad wins a prize. Your raving fans will be rifling through their newspaper looking for you...think of the exposure!

43. Send Birthday and Anniversary Cards

Some businesses are great at collecting birthdays to send their customers deals or specials on the month of their birthday. For some businesses, say a restaurant, you feel comfortable giving your birthdate because you look forward to going out. For mattress stores, it's slightly different in that some folks are not going to give you their date of birth. But, what about the birth of their new bed? Think you could do something with that date?

You betcha!

Year after year, celebrate the incredible sleep they are now getting. You could use the opportunity to send an email or mail a postcard offering a discount on a bedding accessory, to solicit a review, or to ask for referrals. They will be blown away by your thoughtfulness that you remembered such a big event in their lives – the day their sleep changed forever.

44. Got a Story to Tell? Tell your Local Media About It!

One of the absolute best things you could have happen for your business is to get some free PR with a feature story in the local newspaper. But how will they ever know to write about you unless you tell them? Every business has a unique story to tell. Or a unique product they sell or a unique service they offer.

Recently, we contacted the newspaper because we had just put an $18,000 Carpe Diem bed in a local hotel, which I thought was a pretty neat story. Anyone can book that room if they truly wanted to experience luxurious sleep. We typed up a short press release and sent it to the person who handles news stories.

It took a week, but we had a reporter from the newspaper contact us saying they thought it was newsworthy enough to do a story on. Cool enough, but it gets better. Through our conversation with the reporter, we started telling her about some of the unique things that we do and the news story turned into a free advertisement for Gardner's! They highlighted our Dream Room (used a picture of), hyped up our Sleep Easy Workshops, and also talked about the bed in the hotel. This article generated enormous buzz in the community, not to mention a packed house for our workshop, and surging sales.

What story can you tell?

45. Do Something Charitable in the Community

First of all, it just feels good to give back. And no matter which cause you choose, it will be beneficial to you in more ways than one. On such examples goes back a few years. In November of 2012, one of our customers made us aware of a non-profit organization called Holiday Hope. Holiday Hope helps families have a truly wonderful Christmas that otherwise would be left in need during the Holidays. All the children wanted was simply to have a bed to sleep in. Honestly I was moved to tears - in a year in which Ben and I both "gave up" Tempur-Pedic mattresses to enjoy a new Carpe Diem mattress - here was a young child asking for a new bed so he and his brothers, one of which has special needs, wouldn't have to sleep on the floor.

Truly, eye opening and humbling and needless to say, we were more than happy to help these folks out.

Since 2012 Gardner's has helped Holiday Hope each year with their efforts. Beginning in 2017 we began an ongoing all year charitable effort called Gardner's Gives Back. On each delivery we make we ask our customers to contribute at a least one non-perishable food item. Throughout the year we estimate that we will collect over 2,000 pounds of food items. Along with this we make a monthly monetary donation to food banks and animal rescue groups. In truth this is more for us and our belief to give back to the community than it being good for the business but in reality the goodwill created is enormous and pays dividends to our business.

46. Offer Fun and Educational Workshops

Hosting a workshop is a fun way to bring new leads and past customers into your showroom for a night of sleep education. Identify and align yourself with trusted health professionals in your community who have a message to share about sleep. Health professional ideas include:

- Physical Therapists (positioning and pillow selection)
- Sleep Doctors (obvious)
- Dentists (snoring, sleep apnea)
- Chiropractors (spinal health)

It's highly likely that the health professional will be interested in sharing their knowledge with a group who may need their services as well. Typically, it will be a free event for those who attend, but that doesn't mean go cheap. Get it catered, and make your attendees say WOW!

Your prospects will be mingling with your raving fans, turning them into customers quickly. If you video record it, you have some great content to use for other purposes.

47. Interview Customers After Purchase

When do you think is the best time to solicit a review or testimonial from a customer? Hopefully you guessed right after they give you their money, because that's it. It's highly likely that they gave you their business because they trusted you and were overwhelmed by the buying experience you provided. They feel relief that their buying decision has been made and they are excitedly anticipating a good night's sleep. Why wait to solicit a testimonial? They'll be ready to gush about you and about how smart they were to do business with you.

Capture a little video of them. If they aren't open to a video, snap a picture of them and get them to write something about their experience. Then post the videos on YouTube using proper keywords, and post them to your website. When future customers are interested in a product that someone else gave a testimonial for, be quick to use it.

Video testimonials:

48. Write Blog Posts for Search Engine Optimization

We'll never be confused with web developers, but we know enough about what works online to be dangerous. One of the best ninja tricks for getting traffic to your website is to write blog posts for Search Engine Optimization (SEO) purposes.

Blogs get high credibility from the search engines because blogs typically contain the most fresh, unique, and relevant content to your searches. While writing a blog post is easy – it's not just dumping whatever's in your head onto the page, you've got to do it right to get noticed. There are simple rules to follow and believe us, you don't have to be a tech guy to get it.

Some key points to keep in mind are: Use specific keywords you want to target in your headline and multiple times throughout your copy. Keyword rich as they say. Also, the content has to be unique. If content is copied and pasted into your blog, not only is that shady and illegal, but the Google bots don't like it and you won't get traffic.

49. Put a Unique Marketing Message on Your Truck

Look at the delivery trucks your competitors drive around town. I'll bet that all of them are image and brand focused, with the content likely coming directly from their vendors. That means that there is very little differentiation between trucks within a community – how can the public keep anyone straight?

Very little thought is given to that fact that your delivery vehicle is a giant moving billboard driving through the neighborhoods of your future customers. Let that statement sink in. So, why not make your truck stand out with a message that the reader remembers about you. What is one thing you can say on your truck that your competitors can't? What message will get them to follow the truck to your store?

50. Don't Be Afraid To Offer Long Term Financing

Truth is, you can control this more than you think.

We have found that although having a long term offer in our ads is valuable. And when it comes down to it, our customers would rather finance in the 6-24 month period, especially when we offer them this shorter term financing in conjunction with some other bonus items or premiums such as a free mattress protector.

When told that either long term financing OR shorter term financing is available along with a free gift, often our customers will go with the short term and free stuff.

In the end, we win due to the high perceived value of what we give away along with the lower discount rate in the shorter term financing.

51. Steer Clear of Price Games and Deception

Let's face it, people hate mattress shopping. And one of the biggest reasons are the price games and advertising deception that 95% of the industry puts out there. Every weekend there's a reason for another sale! What makes this weekend's "2 day sale" better or different than last week's "door buster" event? Why is last week's "buy it now or the deal is off" price being offered this week too? We ask you, why do you want to contribute to your customer's ire?

If you feel you need to do what everyone else in town does to be competitive, you're wrong. You'll run out of money quickly as your competition has more money to spend, and you'll likely get lost in the clutter anyway. You need to be smarter and stick out with a different message. Be the voice of reason in your market. Pull the sheets back and expose the games that the chain stores play. And tell your prospects what the right way to shop for a mattress is…your way. They'll respect you for it and you'll get the sale. We have a wealth of messages that stick out and we can help you to craft your message.

52. Offer Sleep Assessments

Think about what the first five minutes are like for your prospect when they enter your store. What is their experience? If it's like most stores, where a prospect is greeted with a "can I help you? Oh, you're looking for a mattress? Cool. Come over here and try this bed," you need a new approach. Your chain store competition with their highly trained sales sharks will blow your sales team out of the water if you use that approach.

You need an approach that not only sticks out, but guides your customer to the bed that best suits their sleep needs. I've always heard that the best thing you can do when selling a mattress is to get your prospect to lie down on beds for as long as possible. However, how do you know what beds to show them if you know nothing about their sleep needs? This is where a sleep assessment comes in. I don't have much space here to go into great detail about what the assessment entails, rather to stress the importance of using a sleep assessment.

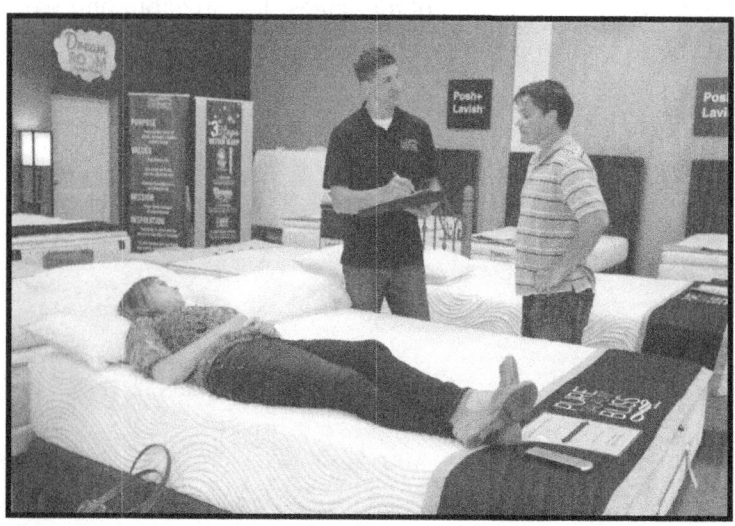

53. Diversify, Don't Be Dependent on One Brand

We cannot stress how important this is, not only for your business health, but your mental stress level too. The stores that are struggling the most right now are ones who have hitched their wagon to one brand. For years, that philosophy worked as there may have been an exclusivity agreement of some kind offering you protection. However, that exclusivity is likely long gone. The chain stores have moved into your territory meaning that you are not the destination for that brand you once were.

Today the gloves are off when it comes to "what once was" and "they way we do things" about selling mattresses. Advances in logistics, online reach and advertising have allowed your vendors to establish direct relationships with your customers.

Regardless of how you feel about the new normal when it comes to consumer relationships and how they purchase their mattress, the number one thing you must do is to always keep your brand, your story top of mind with your customers. Never allow it to be overshadowed by your vendors desires and needs.

While many vendors may disagree with this, given the options consumers have today to purchase directly from almost every vendor in the US, the reality is that most shoppers still enjoy an in-person experience.

It is your job to create a wonderful mattress buying experience backed up with an expertly curated selection of unique, exciting and different mattress options.

54. Dig Deep On Your Local Message

There is no doubt there is power in a locally owned message when told in your marketing messages and advertising. Here is a checklist to ensure that you cover all the bases available when you dig deep on your local marketing message

- [ ] Tell your family story and history – include as many pictures and moments from the archives as possible
- [ ] Use the important words "Family-Owned, Operated and Managed- Daily"
- [ ] Use your picture and your family pictures – caricatures work wonderfully well in lieu of family photos if you wish to maintain a layer of privacy
- [ ] Support other local businesses and let it be known to those owners that you own a local business as well, local business networking is powerful
- [ ] Seek out and find a local referral group to have others refer your business and be a contributing member
- [ ] Support in-state factories whenever possible and when it makes sense on your sales floor. Mattresses made locally in your state is a powerful and connective message
- [ ] Highlight definitive service points and features, don't just take the easy way out and say "our service is better" spell out each service point which is unique or where you have the advantage over others
- [ ] Give back to your community and highlight those efforts in your marketing
- [ ] Highlight any local awards or accolades you have received

55. Show as Many Adjustable Bed Bases as Possible

This one's no-brainer given the sheer volume of advertising dedicated to bed bases today. If you want to increase your average mattress ticket, this is the single easiest way to do it. In most cases, you are DOUBLING your sale. Instead of worrying when the doorbell is going to ring, you need to sell more to the person already in front of you.

Literally every mattress that can be used effectively on an adjustable bed base should be shown on one. But that's only step one. Step two is selling the bed base. The road block with most sales associates is thinking that there is a price hurdle with a customer. The benefits of a bed that is fully customizable to their sleep needs justifies the price.

Remember when value exceeds the price asked, you affirm that the sleep solution prescribed commands the price asked.

The single biggest thing on the sales floor that will impact perceived value is making the customer work too hard to understand what they are about to invest in. In other words, if you have a minimal amount of bed bases on the floor and "grope in the dark" to show this mattress over here, with that bed base along the wall over there it will be very hard to build value that is lasting and permanent in the customer's mind.

While adding bed bases to the floor is an expense it is the single biggest driver in raising your average ticket and increasing sales overall.

56. Sell Unique & Valuable Products

Be different or die. This is a mantra we follow in many aspects. It carries through in our products we offer as well.

We, as consumers, like choice. For us, it has never been about a brand story as it has been more about a better sleep story. We have sought out premium products that deliver on this promise of better health through better sleep. Further, we look for and embrace products that are unique to us and a first in the marketplace that we sell in.

Let's face it, since our business is a just-in-time model, what do you really have to lose trying something different? Your floor model costs are usually subsidized, so why not make an attempt to have something unique that delivers a premium sleep experience? Likewise, when you sell something unique and different that cannot be had elsewhere, you are now able to charge a higher price. Read that last sentence again.

Part 3:
Will Do Tips

57. Always Ask For Testimonials

This is the best social proof you can have. Testimonials are great and give us a customer before they even get to the store. Often, we are told that due to our overwhelming positive reviews and testimonials, our customers knew we were the place to buy from.

Ask for testimonials, and have a process in place to get them. Via our CRM, we are doing a follow-up survey, sending a testimonial form with each delivery, and even getting photos in the store once a sale is made. All a process. All a system.

Of course, we have a very good social media following and a decent amount of them come through our various social media channels. We go one step further, since not everyone will ever see these glowing comments, we screen capture them and create an image. This now gives us a JPEG file to use anywhere and everywhere, and we do.

We post these comments given to us online and use them offline in our newspaper ads, postcards, sales letters, and in our testimonial book at the sales counter. And all of this is done automatically using the CRM system we have built for our business.

Basically, anywhere a testimonial is useful we use them, and have an extensive library of them specific to each brand we sell.

58. Remember "Clean Boots Save Lives"

The title of this chapter is a quote from Gen. Norman Schwarzkopf. He was referring to the fact that a soldier that keeps his boots clean, one of the most basic and simple rules to follow, can be counted on when a life is on the line.

Now, what we do is in no way meant to be compared to the daily threats our armed forces face each day, but rather a point that the little things are important.

We all know that women are the core shoppers and 80% of the time are driving the purchase. So why not have a clean store? Clean the corners, clean under the beds.

Look UP!

Let's face it - the customer does, what are they seeing? Stained tiles due to that water leak last summer? Light bulbs burned out? Cobwebs?

It's funny how the little things can sink a sale, and whether you realize it or not, you are being judged on the appearance of your store. Think about it, how can she trust you to keep her foyer, stairs, hallway, and bedroom clean when you won't keep your own store clean?

59. Have a Designated Play Area for Kids

This seems like it could be a waste of time but frankly it's not. We have a simple area complete with some blocks, books, games, and a Thomas the Train play table that kids just love (all brought from home when our kids outgrew it).

It helps us too. How many times have you been interrupted by the upset or impatient child wanting to go? Give the children something to focus on besides their Mom and Dad and you will buy yourself extra time to present your products and make the sale.

Plus, it keeps them occupied with the toys and not acting out a real life version of monkeys on the bed.

60. No Solicitations without Appointment

Go right now and put it on your front door if it's not there already.

The point of this is to make you realize that your time is valuable. When the doorbell rings and it's anything other than a prospect that might spend money with you, it's likely a waste of your time. Now, that's not to say that you shouldn't meet with anyone. After all, you never know when and from whom the next great idea will come. However, your day must be meticulously scheduled with a prioritized list of items you need to get done and you must stick to your schedule.

Inform your vendor reps, advertising reps, and anyone else that they must schedule an appointment with you. Same goes for the phone. Have your staff inform the caller that you're not available and that they can send you information via email. This way you can digest the information when you want to and respond if necessary.

Don't let your time be wasted!

61. Send Thank You Notes to Your Customers

If you're not sending thank you notes to your customers, you should start. First, it's nice to send a simple thank you message, letting them know that you appreciate their support of your business and that if they need you for any reason, you're available. Second, you can use a "P.S." message to ask for a review or testimonial or even give them some sort of special offer. Don't overwhelm them with a salesy type of message, but offer them something they want. Maybe even offer a free gift if they bring a friend in to Gardner's.

If you systematize and have the staff, a hand written thank you card is best. Nothing says sincerity like a hand written card. If you're like us, you want speed and want it done 100% of the time, so we automate our cards through our CRM. We use special, personalized touches in our message so it looks like we tailored the card special to them, however, it's automated and gets done immediately after we complete their delivery. No hand cramps, no licking envelopes, and no running to the post office. Either method is fine, it just needs to get done.

62. Survey Your Customers for Important Feedback

This is essential and actually easier than you think to do. It is essential because it will let you know what your customers like most about you and what you need to work on or change. Obviously, the "like most about you" things are the items you highlight in your marketing. The critical scores are not to be ignored, nor should any offense be taken from them. If your customers care about you and your business, they will be open and honest with you and often point out things that you do not see.

A survey can be done a few different ways and here are a few ideas: leave a survey on delivery of merchandise with a stamped return envelope, direct them to an online survey (survey monkey is a good one), or have a Virtual Assistant (if you're not familiar with Virtual Assistants, google it!) conduct a phone survey for you and automate the process through a CRM. Some survey ideas include: a survey about their delivery experience, their satisfaction of their mattress, what sleep issues are most common, and how likely they are to refer to you. You may even offer to give them something for completing the survey.

63. Know What Customers are Searching for Online

This sounds challenging, but it's not. Have you ever checked out the free tools that Google has made available for everyone? Did we mention free? Google trends is a simple way to find out what is trending online. Type in any word you'd like to search for and see what's out there. This is an easy and quick way to get relevant blog content.

One of the best tools available is through a Google Adwords account called the Keyword Planner. Google Adwords is a pay per click service offered by Google that I highly recommend. You should have a few Adwords campaign set up for some of your unique brands or services. Set a daily budget and let it go. The Keyword planner will give you an idea of what search terms have high competition and which ones have low which is important because you will want to find some search terms that you can stand out in.

64. Use Google Alerts to Your Advantage

We know you've heard of Google, but you may not know about Google Alerts. Basically, Google Alert allows you to monitor the web for specific content you are interested in.

It can be a daily email sent to your inbox with the most current searches to a keyword you tell Google you want an Alert for. For example, if you set up an Alert for the keyword "mattress," every day you'll get one email with up to 10 searches listed that relates to mattresses.

You can create a Google Alert for as many keywords as you'd like. You definitely should enter your name and your store name because you want to know who's talking about you. Other keywords ideas for Alerts are your brands, your competitors, and other industry buzz words. Knowledge is power and Google Alerts is an easy way to deliver knowledge to your inbox.

Visit www.google.com/alerts.

65. Build a Marketing Peer Network

There is nothing more powerful than having a network of associates who can evaluate and critique your marketing efforts. We have all heard two sets of eyes are better than one. The late, great Napoleon Hill - one the greatest writers in history on the success mindset - helped to pioneer the mastermind concept.

Simply put, a "Mastermind session" is when two or more people gather to discuss new ideas to generate, acquire, and convert new customers. Many other avenues can be discussed and directions taken, but every mastermind we have been a part of over the years, the core conversation and focus usually comes back to this.

Join an established network, or if you can't find one, create one. Eat lunch once a week with another local business owner and bring along your latest ad or idea and ask them what they think about. Of course, reciprocity is always nice so offer to help them with the same.

A fresh pair of eyes will always be beneficial and I would strongly suggest a pair of eyes outside of your own four walls and industry. Look to those that have no idea of what it is you do or sell, have them analyze your marketing piece and make sure they are very clear on what it is you are asking them to do if they were your customer.

66. Give Everyone a Story to Behold and Be Told

The single biggest payoff for a business owner is when they are referred to family and friends by happy customers. The key here is to best manage the story you wish your happy customers to tell others.

What story have you given your customer to "behold" in their experience with you, and then how are you enabling them to pass along the story that is told to their friends and family?

Will they talk about price, service, product, you and your staff? Well, I can tell you none of that really matters to person being referred to you by your customer.

They want, what they want – not what their friend got.

But, if you can give your customers a story to be told, deliver them a script or better yet a pass along to hand to their friends and family members even better. Our **7 Step Wake Up Happy Promise** is the cornerstone of our marketing plan and everything we do dovetails into these seven steps. Each step is easily understood and easily told all while answering what's in it for me as a new potential customer.

**Download a Copy of Our
7 Step Wake Up Happy Promise!**

To get a copy of our Promise and other examples we show in this book, go to:

www.RenegadeMattressRetailer.com/bonuses

---

67. Follow and Study Other Successful Local Businesses

While you should certainly follow your competition, you should know what is going on in with other businesses within your community too. Facebook is the easiest way to do this, but going through the business section of your local paper is another. You never know what great idea might come along that you can implement in your business as a result of studying another business. Many of the great things we do at Gardner's are things we studied, copied, and implemented from other great businesses.

There's not much that's new anymore, so you need to stay alert and don't be afraid to try something new to you and make it a success. For example, our Private Mattress Consultation concept is a result of studying the process a patient goes through with a health professional. Our thought is, why should sleep be any different? We took the appointment idea, tweaked it for mattresses, and it's working with great results.

68. Put Yourself Out There, Don't Hide

People buy from other people they like, plain and simple. This is true with us. We're more apt to buy from a business where we feel like we know the business owner. We may never meet them, but we know that if there is an issue, that there is someone to talk to. Also, people like being part of your success story.

When it comes down to buying a bed at $1,999 from a faceless chain store or buying the same bed at the same price from Ben and Jeff at Gardner's Mattress & More, which store do you think gets the business? We'll even argue that the customer is willing to spend more to spend it with someone they know, like, and trust. Put your name and picture on your marketing, your website, and in your store. Make sure your prospects and customers know who you are and that you care deeply about them?

Get to know Gardner's...

I'd like you to trust your sleep to Gardner's. However, that is an unrealistic expectation if you don't know and trust us first. Here's a sneak peek at the people you'll run into at Gardner's:

Ben McClure, co-owner   Jeff Giagnocavo, co-owner

69. Have an Informational Facebook Page

If you're looking to Facebook to be your main source of traffic, you're looking in the wrong place. Facebook is one of many places to find a customer, but it's much more organic than traditional forms of advertising. Facebook, enables you to cultivate trust and build relationships with your followers and their friends in an non-salesy way.

But just having a Facebook page and asking people to "like" is not enough. You have to have some fun, share sleep tips and relevant mattress content they want to read, and run contests. You should post something daily, but it should not always be about your store and most definitely not "salesy." Maybe about 15% of the time you can mention specials and events, but the rest should be fun, informational stuff. And by all means, post every good review and testimonial you get. Social proof reaps huge dividends.

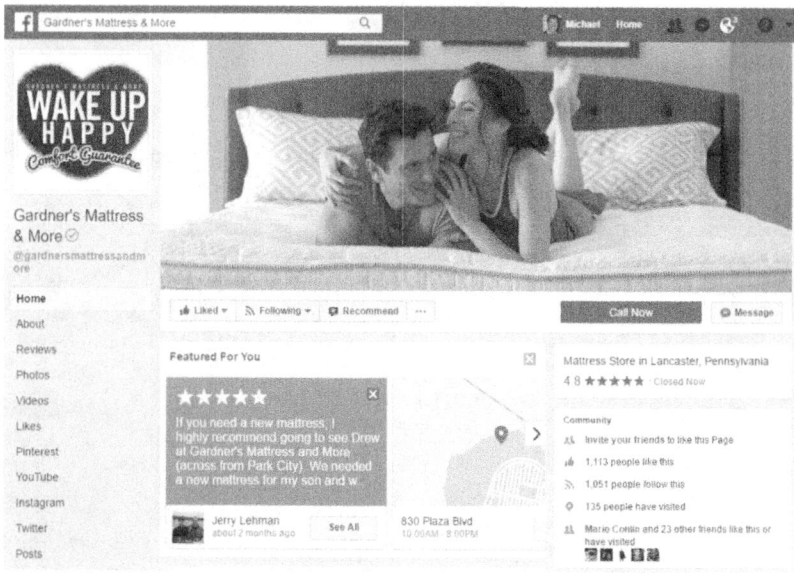

70. Hire Picketers to "Protest" Your Store

This is a fun one, and certainly an example of outrageous advertising. Hire the same people you would if you wanted a sign walker/holder. Create a sign or signs "protesting" your store on any one of the following points:

- Fair and honest pricing
- Outstanding customer service
- Incredible results
- No more back pain
- No more stiff and sore muscles
- Cares about my sleep
- Service after the sale

Or make up your own. The idea here is to create a visible flash mob experience so the people driving by your store get the message that you are a great choice to purchase from and you beg their attention.

71. Do Off-Beat Promotions

This kind of goes back the statement of you are selling yourself first and your products second. We have done Festivus promotions - the holiday made famous by the show Seinfeld, Guest TV star promotions (yes, a real ABC television star - Charlie McDermott from The Middle) local baseball team promotions, and even "the boss is away" promotions in order to sell off floor model inventory.

We even tie in some of our personal beliefs with the holidays. For instance on the 4th of July we give away a copy of the U.S. Constitution and tie this into our advertising too.

Think of something fun and promote it. The more fun, the more outrageous, the better. Remember, we sell mattresses. It's really not that serious - we aren't launching rockets into space or have a finger on the nuke button. Have some fun with your next promotion.

Charlie McDermott (Axl from ABC's hit show The Middle) visited Gardner's and we made a big deal out of it.

72. Take & Use Photographs

The use of photographs in marketing is typically under-utilized by business owners and it's a mistake. Photos are a great way to convey customer-success and they are an excellent tactic to engage people and help build the "know, like and trust factor."

You don't have to go to the expense of hiring a professional photographer to use photos in your business (however for certain types of photos that might be necessary) and often-times the more "down and dirty" approach of a simple cellphone photo is more effective and realistic.

Here are several different types of photos you can use in your mattress marketing efforts:

- Pictures of you in various poses
- Pictures of happy customer right after they bought
- Pictures of your store
- Before and after photos of a good night's sleep
- Enlarged photos detailing specific products
- Pictures of you with happy customers
- Pictures of employees
- Historical or legacy photos of your business
- Pictures of you doing interacting with visitors
- Picture of you having fun
- Picture of your family

73. Have Fun - Host a Contest

Being in business is first and foremost about making money, but you're allowed to have a little fun too. And contests are fun! Running a contest is a great way to generate an enormous amount of leads is a short period of time. You can easily run contests on Facebook with the help of a proper CRM (customer relationship management) system, but you can also run contests in the newspaper (via a mail in entry form), and in your store.

You can run small, monthly giveaways like "enter here to win a free pillow or premium sheet set" or a big one like "win a free $1999 mattress" during an anniversary event. Don't be so concerned with the cost of the giveaway (you might even get a vendor to pony up the free mattress if you ask them nicely!), think more in terms of what you can do with the names you collect.

That's the key to making contests work. If all you do is collect names and give something away to one person, you've defeated the purpose of the contest. After someone enters, they should get an email thanking them for entering. Maybe a day later they get an email about the services you offer. Maybe you send them a postcard or letter.

After the contest ends, send the non-winners an email or letter telling them they didn't win, BUT give them something else for taking part in your contest. Maybe it's a $5 gift card for coming back to the store or a $ OFF certificate if they use it by X/X/XX date. And you should communicate with them till they buy from you.

74. Offer Quality Upgrades & Profit

The easiest way to make money is to sell more when the wallet is already out. Period. There is no easier way, yet so many mattress store owners simply refuse to acknowledge this and if you are one of them, there is money being left on the table.

We presently offer five different mattress protectors, all with its own purpose and selling story. From basic protection to temperature regulating capabilities, we cover all the bases. And guess what, we don't give them away, we sell them all at premium prices.

We offer 10 different styles of sheet sets and over 25 different pillow options too.

All of these items we sell on a regular basis and yes, a successful program does require stock, but not enough to be a burden on inventory dollars or cash flow. We had to establish a rate of sale, but that only took about 4-6 weeks and from there we were off to the races.

This is a service to the customer and something we can sell easily and attach at a high rate. Plus the profit is very nice too.

75. Merchandise Your Bedding Accessories

For as much thought as we all give to our floor and mattress line-ups, it is surprising to me how little we as an industry spend merchandising our accessories. It makes sense doesn't it? Yet how many types of protectors do you offer, one? Quality levels of sheet sets, one? Pillow types, just memory foam and maybe that cheap fiber filled giveaway?

It's no wonder that Bed Bath Beyond and the like eat our lunch when it comes to accessories. Yes, they have volume purchasing power that we can sometimes only shake our head at. But at the end of the day, our customers all have two budgets in mind when purchasing a mattress set.

The first is for the mattress. The second, and the one you rarely know of, or up until now didn't even consider, is everything else they are changing in the bedroom. This includes sheets, pillows, comforters, carpet, paint, window treatments, lamps, and more.

Now, we are not saying go out and get paint and carpet to offer. But do have a well thought out merchandising plan when it comes to accessories. The budget is there, the customer's mind has already spent the money - it's up to you simply let them know you have a great selection of accessories.

Our mattress protection line offers five different protectors ranging from basic to the ultimate in cool sleep technology. We even offer a money back guarantee on our top end offerings. If they don't work our customers can bring them back, no questions asked. We simply give them the difference between the premium protector and the basic one, and they leave with the basic one in hand.

Guess what? We have never been stung by this, and sure, we've had a few returns, but the margins we get on our top end protector $249/queen more than makes up for it from everyone else that keeps it. Same can be said for sheets and pillows. We absolutely love the DreamFit sheet program. They are a great company and their program offers unique features that just are not found elsewhere. Plus, they offer seven different types of sheet sets and mattress protection too, which we use for our top end offering.

Pillows, we have them all. At last count we have over 25 different types of pillows, and it at times seems like a little much, but we sure do sell them and customers love the fact that we offer such a great selection.

76. Uniformity is Important for First Impressions

We have decided it is best to have our delivery staff in uniforms. Gone are the days of employees coming in with faded blue jeans and t-shirts. They've been replaced with quality branded uniforms that deliver a touch point, the last one too by the way, which our customers appreciate. So much of what we work for can be undone by the littlest of things.

This includes your delivery staff. Our uniforms are supplied by Uni-First, a cost effective source that has made it very easy to have our staff uniformed. We even split the cost 50/50 with our employees as they see it as a benefit since they are not ruining their clothes and saving time on laundry. Likewise, we have peace of mind knowing that our employees aren't wearing a shirt with a message on it that is less than impressive of our company.

77. Customer Delivery – Do Something With It!

This is more than uniforms. It is your last touch point with your customer during a sale. Properly training your staff on how to handle objections and issues that may arise are important. Of course, we do our best to set all expectations and answer all potential questions at the point of sale. But sometimes things come up, and when they do, our staff is trained to simply reply with "That is not a problem, I'm going to call the store now and have you speak with one of the owners or your sales person"

Don't get me wrong, this doesn't happen all the time, but it's nice to know we handle it properly when these issues arise.

But more importantly, our problems are mitigated by how our delivery staff engages the customer. We are never pushy, offer a two hour delivery window, call ahead if we will be early or late, and wear protective shoe coverings to make sure we don't scuff or soil the floor.

Yes, all of this does take extra time. But it is time well spent. There is nothing worse than making your delivery constraints a problem for your customer. Plus, think about it - our customer is not only inviting someone into their home, but into their bedroom. A very private place. To us, it makes sense to make the delivery process as easy and stress free as possible.

77 Tips...
Use Them and Grow Rich!

Congratulations on making it to the end of all 77 tips. It is my sincere hope you implement most, if not all, of these powerful profit-makers.

Before you put this book down, I want to invite you to learn a bit more about how my team and I can help you increase your mattress sales and profitability.

Our company is dedicated to helping independent mattress retailers thrive and prosper in their local community.

We have proven strategies to effectively compete against the Big Box and online retailers.

Check out the next few pages and make the commitment to join us!

Suggested Resources from Jeff Giagnocavo

Amplify Your Mattress Sales

In addition to our two retail stores, my business partners and I have a consulting company where we help the independent mattress retailer sell more mattresses and add-on's.

Period.

Our mission is to help the independent mattress retailer to become THE PLACE to buy a mattress in his or her community; enable them to compete with and outsmart the Big Box and direct-to-consumer Internet retailers; and allow them increase profits and decrease ad spend.

We are mattress retailers like you, but with a profound difference.

When I purchased a failing local mattress retail business in Lancaster, PA back in 2011, my business partner Ben and I "blew up" the business, and other than keeping the customer list, we started from scratch and built something entirely new.

We didn't look within the stale, "been there, done that" mattress retail world for inspiration.

Instead, we started by researching stellar customer service companies outside the mattress retail space. We then built a foundation from proven direct response marketing strategies. On top of those we built a cutting-edge marketing automation technology platform to create a radically NEW blueprint for the mattress retail business we wanted to have, and our customers would love!

We didn't build a mattress retail business - we reinvented the mattress retail business.

One of the "secrets" we uncovered back in 2011 seems simple, yet is profound. In order to reinvent the culture inside a business' four walls, you must reinvent and makeover what the business is all about - to your customers, your staff, your community and most importantly to you the owner.

If we simply took over and ran the business "as-is", nobody, including our potential customers, would be excited by it; and if we simply ran it like any one of the other 137 mattress retailers in our local community, we would be, for all intents and purposes, invisible.

Over the past five years, Ben and I have been innovators and pioneers when it comes to selling mattresses and competing with the big box retailers and online retailers. More importantly, we've taken a decidedly different approach to sharing our successes and have an open door, do not hold anything back philosophy.

A couple visiting our store and reading our mattress buying guides while trying out different mattresses.

Our world-famous Dream Room™ allows prospects to try out the mattress of their choice in a private, luxury hotel-like room for a few hours.

Our unique information-first retailing model, combined with exceptional customer service has resulted in our growth, year after year!

This openness to sharing, in and of itself, is a radical change in our industry and one we are proud to offer you. Our mantra is *"a rising tide lifts all ships"* and if we can help other independent mattress retailers model our success, we, as an industry, can only get stronger.

We believe the independent mattress retailer is an important and vital part of our local community and national history, which NO Big Box chain or internet-based company can take away or compete with.

We help mattress retailers who:

- Complete against big box and department stores
- Feel like they are always justifying their store versus other stores
- Have customers always looking for a deal
- Wish their customers would refer more actively and give more five star reviews online
- Would like customers to move away from the cheapest thing possible and truly invest in a quality sleep system

Connect with us:

If you want to discover our "secret sauce" for creating a mattress retail business that is fun and innovative, contact us for a private, fact-finding strategy call.

Thank you for reading this far and to your success!

Jeff Giagnocavo
888-688-1974
470 Boot Rd. #688, Downingtown, PA 19335
jeff@renegademattressretailer.com

Renegade Reviews

The value Jeff and his team are giving to the bedding industry is special. Renegade Mattress Retailer Weekly is packed with practical tips and ideas that will help retailers realize their unique competitive advantage in their respective market (if they put it into practice). This isn't arm chair phycology. This is powerful & tactical information created for retails by real life retail practitioners.

Doug Stewart
Director of Training
MEGA Group USA

Renegade Mattress Retailer Weekly is a great way for people selling mattresses to stay sharp and learn from others who are having some success. Jeff and his team aren't business consultants; they are actual bedding retailers that live the business every day. You can't go wrong if your goal is to serve the consumer, and RMRW delivers great content to help you do that.

Mark Quinn
President of Spink & Edgar USA

Renegade Mattress Retailer Weekly

Renegade Mattress Retailer Weekly is a **free**, weekly, digital newsletter (delivered to your inbox or cell phone your choice) published for independent mattress retailers by independent mattress retailers.

Every issue of Renegade Mattress Retailer Weekly is designed to give you specific and immediately usable ideas and strategies to boost mattress and add-on sales, which are working in our stores and the stores of other successful mattress retailers.

Each issue is designed to be watched or read in less than 10 minutes, so that you can take what we are giving you and quickly do something with it.

If you are looking for fresh and innovative ideas to attract more customers and sell more mattresses and add-on's, you must subscribe to Renegade Mattress Retailer Weekly!

Get Renegade Mattress Retailer Weekly For FREE!

Sign up today by visiting:

www.RenegadeMattressRetailer.com

Test-Drive the Renegade Mattress Retailer Inner Circle

The Renegade Mattress Retailer Inner Circle (RMRIC) is the place where success oriented mattress retailers belong and where they go to be inspired, connect and profit from our insights and the collective peer group that resides with the Renegade Mattress Retailer Inner Circle.

Membership isn't for everyone. If free advice is the only advice you seek, this isn't the place. If membership were free no one would put value on it and we would have a very poor group of sad-sack retailers crying "woe is me" all the time.

Instead we have put together an amazing, and growing by the day, group of retailers who are looking for the slightest edge to make new sales, improve profits, decrease their ad spend and ultimately discover how to have a business that works for them, so they can finally get out of the store once and for all.

Get all the details about the Renegade Mattress Retailer Inner Circle by visiting:

www.RenegadeMattressRetailer.com

A couple visiting our store and perusing through our library of helpful mattress buying guides.

The #1 Strategy That Changed It All For Us

If asked, I could easily point to one, simple strategy that took our mattress retail business from good to great, and more importantly one that you can easily add to your business and get the same results we have.

What is this strategy you ask?

Information-first retailing or Infotail as we call it.

Information-first retailing is a customer-centric strategy that puts the focus on helping before selling, and specifically uses strategically-designed educational tools to attract qualified leads.

Our philosophy is you don't need to trick customers with fancy graphics, deceptive ads, price schemes, and scare tactics. Give them your best "stuff" up front and be completely transparent. This information-based approach has led to the development of the core Infotail tool – the educational mattress buying guides and the automated follow-up systems built around these unique short books.

We've invested hundreds of hours and tens-of-thousands of dollars perfecting our buying guides for our stores and our clients' stores.

These short books build trust between you and your prospective customer by delivering educational information about your products and services. It says exactly what you want to say to your leads and crafts the sales presentation. It's your voice. It shows them the exact path you want them to follow and shortens the sales cycle. It eliminates confusion and the need to shop around. It's not salesy. And it's a breath of fresh air in an industry with high levels of consumer frustration.

These guides are the foundation of ALL our marketing and we offer them in everything that we create to get prospects to walk in our door. We use them as online lead generation devices to exchange contact information for the guides, and we hand out at expos and home shows. They are also great takeaways when someone wants to go home and think about their purchase.

Information-first marketing is an important and strategic strategy that provides several unique benefits to consumers and to you, including:

- A help-before-you-sell process
- A trust-building tool which alleviate concerns/skepticism
- Positioning you as the local expert for getting the right mattress

The concept of information-first marketing is not new, and if you look back on the history of mattress industry, you can see examples as far back as 1901, when the Ostermoor Company published the book, "The Test of Time," which contained "144 pages of vital importance to anyone who values health and long life, and the restful sleep that insures both."

You might think that a strategy used over 100 years ago would be outdated and not work in today's attention-deficit society, which would be flat-out inaccurate.

Our buyer's guides are designed to attract the right type of consumer – one is who **informed, educated and knows the value of good night's sleep.**

They are not brochures, nor do they contain brochure-like language. There's specialized marketing "science" in these guides, including benefit-laden copywriting that sets up your prospects to become informed, and most importantly deliver them great value about a confusing topic that everybody hates to do and that's buying a mattress.

When done right, the consumer views you as the authority and they come in to your store ready to buy from you.

Here are five reasons educational buyer's guides are critically important for mattress retailers:

1. They help before you sell
2. They are a unique marketing & lead generation tool - those who have read your shook spend more, are better clients, and refer more
3. They set your business apart and ahead of your competition - you are the local expert on sleep
4. They increase sale tickets and add-on sales
5. They are a powerful referral and pass along tool

We can help you tap into the amazing power of being a published author of your own mattress buying guides. Automatic Mattress Customers is a unique, cost-effective way to put our expertise to work in your store.

Keep reading for details about this special opportunity.

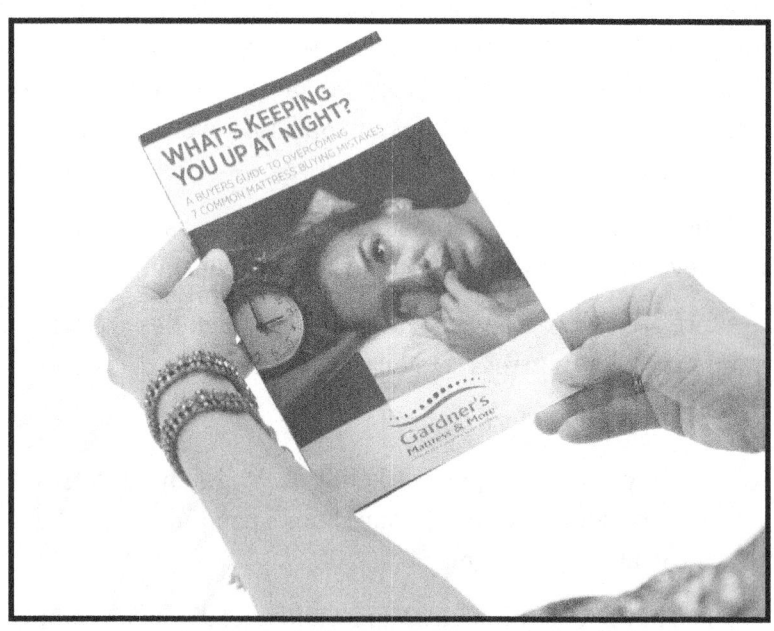

Our mattress buying guides set our stores above the competition in a unique and helpful way.

Automatic Mattress Customers

Automatic Mattress Customers is a turnkey system for independent mattress retailers to attract qualified, ready-to-buy now customers with our proven information-first model.

Automatic Mattress Customers combines the power of our expertly-written buying guides along with an automatic follow-up software solution that makes sure people who have expressed interest in your business hear from you.

These buying guides position you as a local expert and shine a bright, unique light on your store. Customized for your specific business, our buying guides can be both downloaded from your web site and printed and distributed in-store.

Automatic follow-up is an important and strategic goal for you and your business, and it's our goal to help you achieve this enviable opportunity, which eludes most retailers. Automatic Mattress Customers includes a CRM system designed to get people who have downloaded your buying guides into your store.

Automatic Mattress Customers leaves nothing up to chance and you have the peace-of-mind knowing every interested person is being followed-up with to ensure their happiness and your profitability.

Automatic Mattress Customers gives you a pathway to get more people to buy without spending more money on advertising/promotions and automatically without daily thought, work or effort.

Automatic Mattress Customers allows you to replicate yourself as the owner; how you sell; how you follow-up, etc.

Automatic Mattress Customers gives you the opportunity to have unique, segmented marketing lists, based on previous actions or in-actions for future personalized marketing efforts. Check out what one of our customers has to say about the Automatic Mattress Customer process....

> **Gardner's Mattress & More**
> 830 Plaza Blvd.
> Lancaster, PA 17601
> (behind Park City Mall)
>
> **Debra, before our delivery crew departs** we ask that you take just a couple of minutes to let us know how we did. It is our goal to constantly deliver exceptional service.
>
> We would love it if you could tell us whether we did a great job or not. We truly value your opinion of our service and if you are not 100% happy, do not hesitate to let us know on this sheet or call the store immediately.
>
> Your comments are valuable to us and we appreciate them, so let's begin...
>
> Tell us what you thought of _Pete_. How did he do helping you select the right mattress?
> _Willing to give information and educate on various mattresses, how they are made, materials, etc._
>
> What did you think of our process to best assess your sleep needs and suggest the proper mattress?
> _Excellent. I never felt pressured, was never hurried. The concept of a "sleep" room to try out a mattress is good. No sales technique to get me to buy before walking out the door._
>
> One last question Debra. How was your overall experience at Gardner's and would you refer others to Gardner's Mattress & More?
> _My experience is excellent and I have been telling my friends. One of them already bought on my recommendation. Delivery team was very courteous - loved the "goody" bag._
>
> **THANK YOU!**
>
> Debra please accept this small token of thanks for being a great customer and may this $2 bill bring you lots of fortune. Enjoy your new mattress, sleep well!
>
> Debra Metzger
>
> _Great customer service! You are doing it right._

For more details on **Automatic Mattress Customers**, visit:

www.RenegadeMattressRetailer.com

Automatic Mattress Profits

Automatic Mattress Profits is a total, turnkey solution for automating your mattress store so that every Lead, Prospect, Customer, Fan and Friend are followed-up with the way they should be.

There are five critically important systems which should be automated for every mattress retail business looking to fully leverage the marketing automation technology available today.

It should come as no surprise these five follow-up systems align perfectly with the five audiences you have in your business (see tip #1 on page 12).

Trust me, if you get these five follow-up marketing systems up and running and working for you 365 days a year, you are going to see amazing things happen.

More Leads will become Prospects.

More Prospects will become Customers.

More Customers will become Fans.

AUTOMATICALLY!

We have developed a turnkey solution, Automatic Mattress Profits (AMP), for independent mattress retailers to ensure these follow-up systems are in place and automated, so they happen 100% of the time.

We built AMP for our retail stores and it is the result of years of research and development and a $200,000 + investment. The result is nothing short of phenomenal and now you can tap into all the blood, sweat and tears we put into AMP.

AMP includes these five distinct systems:

- Lead Generation System
- Prospect Visit Follow-Up System
- New Customer Follow-Up System
- Fan Follow-Up System
- Friend Nurture System

The Lead Generation Follow-Up System - The purpose of this system is to have an effective sequence of touchpoints to get a qualified Lead to visit or call you. This is the only call-to-action and special incentives may be offered to make this happen.

Prospect Visit Follow-Up System - The implementation of this system requires you to have a thorough assessment so that when a person visits your business, you can determine their specific needs and wants. Then, during the automated follow-up, various tools are used to remind them why they need to take action - based on the criteria uncovered during the assessment.

New Customer Follow-Up System - This system thanks your Customer via email and letter, delivers important order details and fulfillment instructions and if applicable, can deliver a behavioral-based comeback or related offer to them.

Fan Follow-Up System - This unique follow-up system allows for the identification of individuals who are likely to offer positive reviews and referrals, while also giving you a pre-emptive opportunity to follow-up with a Customer who may not be 100% satisfied.

Friend Nurture System - Any of the four audiences, Leads, Prospects, Customers and Fans can go into the Friend Nurture System. Remember, it's not their responsibility to remember you, it is your responsibility to remember them and stay in touch with them.

AMP leaves nothing up to chance and you have the peace-of-mind knowing every Lead, Prospect, Customer and Fan is being followed-up with to ensure their happiness and your profitability.

AMP gives you a pathway to get more people to buy without spending more money on advertising/promotions and automatically without daily thought, work or effort.

AMP allows you to replicate yourself as the owner; how you sell; how you follow-up, etc.

AMP gives you the opportunity to have unique, segmented marketing lists, based on previous actions or in-actions for future personalized marketing efforts.

AMP offers you a proven blueprint to get more positive reviews and build overwhelming social proof (way more than just saying "Like us on Facebook").

AMP is easy to use and can be easily mastered by your staff.

For more details on **Automatic Mattress Profits**, visit:

www.RenegadeMattressRetailer.com

What It Means to be a Renegade Mattress Retailer

Being a Renegade Mattress Retailer is about having a unique direct and intentional philosophy regarding the purpose of your mattress retail business and why it truly exists – to make money and to create owner autonomy. Being profitable and having the business you want to run enables Renegade Mattress Retailers to truly serve their local community and take care of customers at the highest level.

Renegade Mattress Retailers are professionals at the art and craft of giving their customers a great night's sleep. Amateurs they are not.

Renegade Mattress Retailers succeed because of the things they do differently from the masses -including their peers and competitors (key words: "do differently"). They do things their way, but understand the value watching and emulating what other smart business owners do.

Renegade Mattress Retailers make money differently than their peers too - quicker, easier and in bigger chunks than the average retailer. They attract money, rather than pursue it, and strive to achieve real wealth, security and independence.

Renegade Mattress Retailers understand autonomy empowers…

- You to do what you want
- You to do when you want
- You to work with who you want
- At the price, you want
- At the terms, you want

Being a Renegade Mattress Retailer is not about the sleazy sales tactics that have plagued our industry for so long. It's about prioritizing what's most important in your business and setting up systems to achieve them.

If all this resonates with you, you are in the right place and we look forward to having you with us!

Made in United States
North Haven, CT
08 August 2025

71473173R00068